Copyright © 2025 Wild Orbit Books. All rights reserved.
No part of this publication may be copied, reproduced, stored in a retrieval system, or transmitted in any form or by any means—electronic, mechanical, photocopying, recording, or otherwise—without the prior written permission of Wild Orbit Books, except in the case of brief quotations for review or educational purposes.
This book is published by Wild Orbit Books, an independent publishing label dedicated to creative, original storytelling. All characters and events in this publication—unless otherwise stated—are fictitious. Any resemblance to real persons, living or dead, is purely coincidental.
Published by Wild Orbit Books

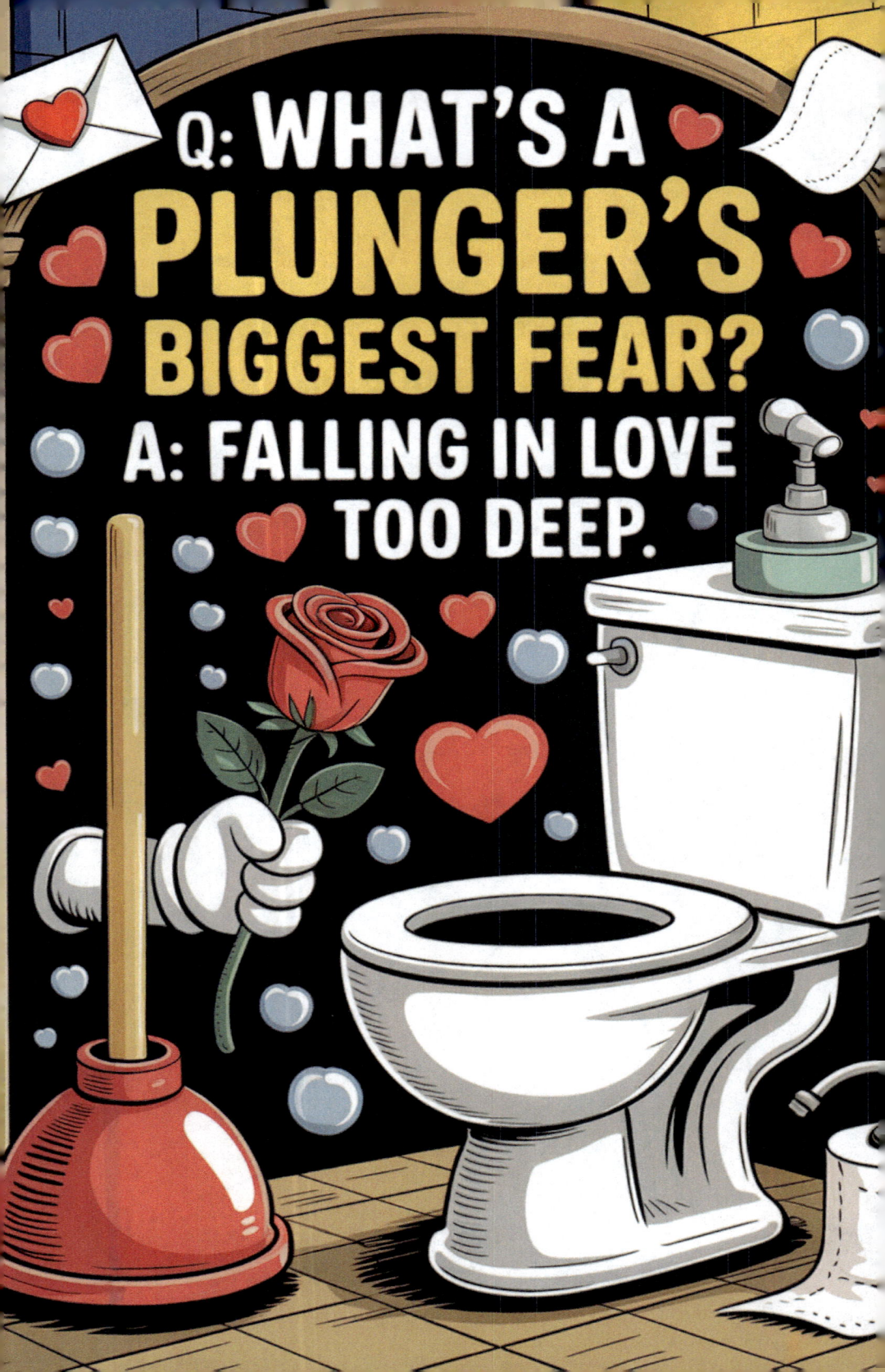

WHY WAS THE MATH BOOK ALWAYS SO TENSE? BECAUSE IT HAD TOO MANY PROBLEMS, AND HONESTLY, SOME OF THEM WERE PRETTY HARD TO SOLVE.

MY LOVE LIFE IS LIKE A BROKEN PENCIL... POINTLESS, AND SOMETIMES, A LITTLE TOO MUCH LEAD GETS INVOLVED.

WHAT'S THE DIFFERENCE BETWEEN A DIRTY BUS STOP AND A LOBSTER WITH BREAST IMPLANTS? ONE'S A CRUSTY BUS STATION, THE OTHER'S A BUSTY CRUSTACEAN.

I TOLD MY WIFE SHE WAS DRAWING HER EYEBROWS TOO HIGH. SHE LOOKED SURPRISED.

WHY DID THE POLICE OFFICER GIVE THE PROSTITUTE A TICKET? SHE WAS CAUGHT SOLICITING A RIDE WITH AN EXPIRED METER.

MY GIRLFRIEND TOLD ME TO TAKE THE SPIDERS OUT INSTEAD OF KILLING THEM. SO I DID. WE HAD A NICE DINNER.

What's the difference between a diplomat and a lady? When a diplomat says yes, he means 'maybe'; when a lady says yes, she means 'yes'. But when a diplomat says maybe, he means 'no'; when a lady says maybe, she means 'no'. When a diplomat says no, he is no diplomat; when a lady says no, she is no lady.

I ASKED MY DOCTOR IF I COULD HAVE SEX WITH MY NEW HIP. HE SAID, "ONLY IF YOU CAN GET IT UP THERE."

WHY DID THE MAN BRING A LADDER TO THE BAR? HE HEARD THE DRINKS WERE ON THE HOUSE, AND HE WANTED TO GET REALLY HIGH.

MY THERAPIST TOLD ME TO EMBRACE MY FLAWS. I GAVE HER A HUG, BUT SHE STILL CHARGED ME FOR THE SESSION.

"MY DATING PROFILE SAYS I'M LOOKING FOR SOMEONE WHO CAN HOLD A CONVERSATION. AND A LOT OF OTHER THINGS."

MY EX SAID I WAS IMMATURE.
I TOLD HER TO GET OUT OF MY
BLANKET FORT.

I ASKED MY SPIRITUAL GUIDE FOR ADVICE ON MY LOVE LIFE. HE JUST SAID, "YOU'VE GOT TOO MUCH BAGGAGE, AND FRANKLY, SOME OF IT LOOKS A BIT USED."

WHY DID THE POLICE OFFICER STOP THE ICE CREAM TRUCK? BECAUSE IT HAD A LOT OF SWEET STUFF IN THE BACK AND WAS DRIVING SUSPICIOUSLY SLOW.

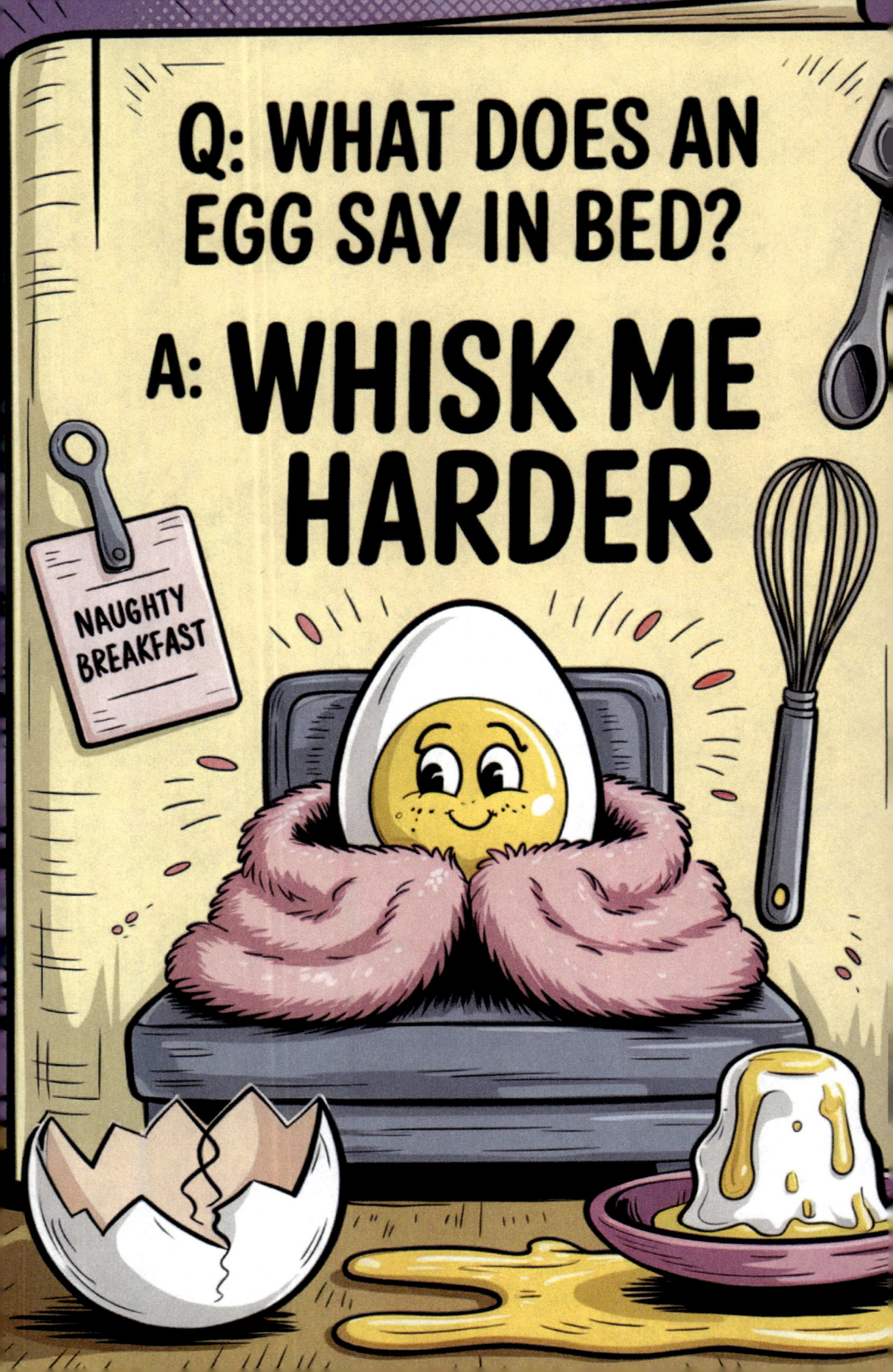

MY GIRLFRIEND SAID SHE NEEDED MORE SPACE. I TOLD HER THE GARAGE WAS FREE, BUT SHE WASN'T IMPRESSED.

WHAT'S THE DIFFERENCE BETWEEN A PIZZA AND A SEX OFFENDER? A PIZZA CAN FEED A FAMILY OF FOUR.

"I LIKE MY COFFEE LIKE I LIKE MY JOKES: DARK AND POSSIBLY INAPPROPRIATE."

I WENT TO A FANCY DRESS PARTY AS A SERIAL KILLER. IT WAS A KILLER OUTFIT, BUT NOBODY REALLY GOT IT.

WHY DID THE SCARECROW WIN AN AWARD? BECAUSE HE WAS OUTSTANDING IN HIS FIELD, AND HE REALLY KNEW HOW TO CULTIVATE A GOOD TIME.

MY DOCTOR TOLD ME I NEED TO STOP THINKING ABOUT SEX. I TOLD HIM I'D HAVE TO UNPLUG FROM THE INTERNET FIRST.

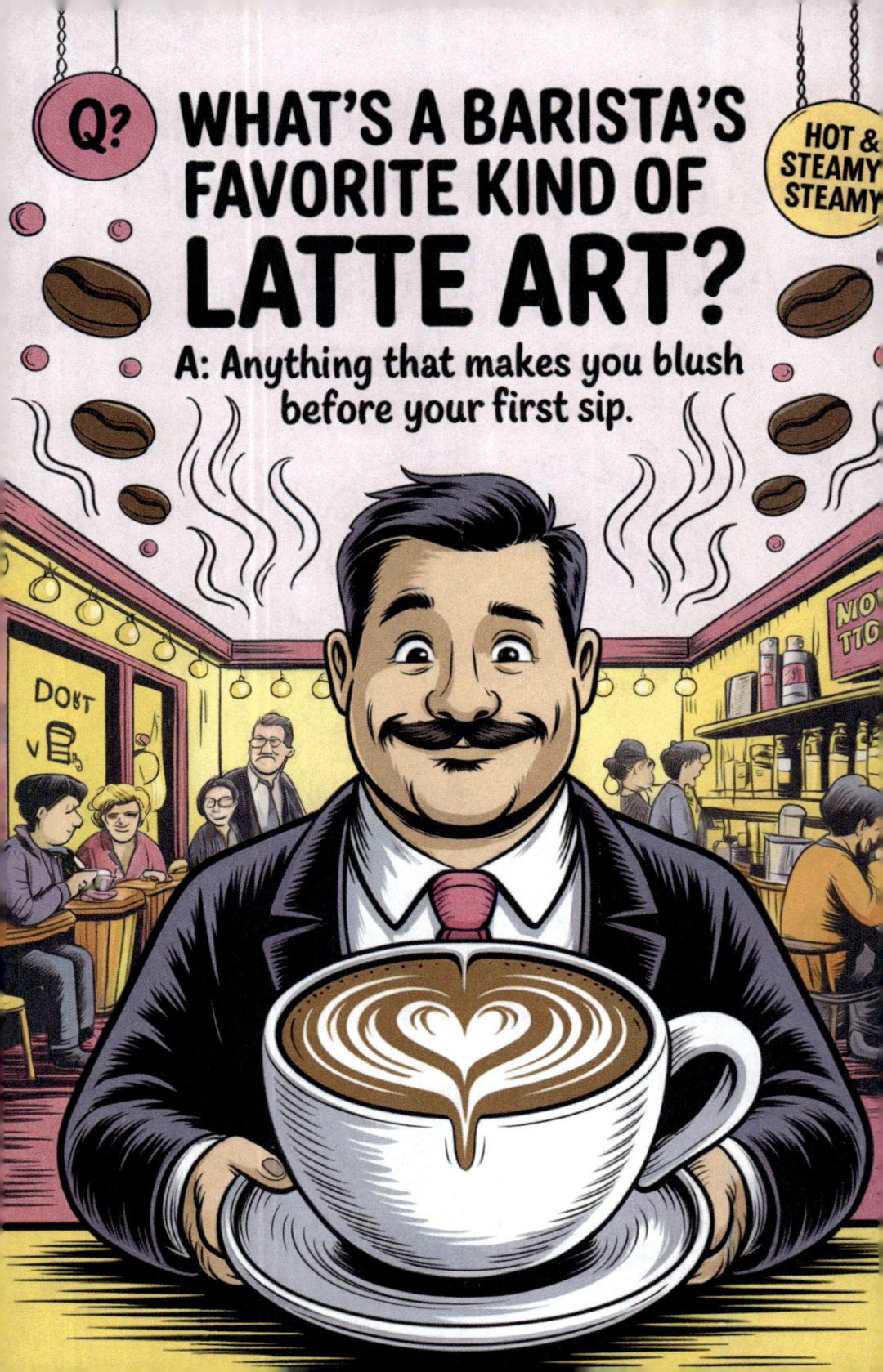

WHAT'S THE BEST WAY TO GET A ONE-ARMED MAN OUT OF A TREE? WAVE TO HIM.

I TRIED TO MAKE A JOKE ABOUT A BROKEN CONDOM, BUT IT JUST FELL FLAT.

MY EX JUST UNFRIENDED ME ON FACEBOOK. I GUESS SHE PREFERS HER HISTORY UN-LIKED.

I TOLD MY WIFE I NEEDED MORE PASSION IN OUR RELATIONSHIP. SHE SUGGESTED I TRY ONLINE DATING, JUST FOR PRACTICE.

WHY DID THE POLICE OFFICER ARREST THE NAKED MAN? HE WAS CHARGED WITH INDECENT EXPOSURE TO THE ELEMENTS.

MY DOCTOR SAID I NEEDED TO CUT DOWN ON MY DRINKING. I TOLD HIM I'D RATHER CUT DOWN ON MY CLOTHES, IT'S MORE FUN.

Q: What's a personal trainer's favorite exercise to "spot" you on?
A: the one that makes you sweat in all the right places.

WHAT'S THE DIFFERENCE BETWEEN A NEW HUSBAND AND A NEW DOG? AFTER A YEAR, THE DOG IS STILL EXCITED TO SEE YOU.

I ASKED MY GIRLFRIEND IF SHE WAS HAVING AN AFFAIR. SHE SAID, "NO, WHAT MAKES YOU THINK THAT?" I SAID, "WELL, YOU'RE LOOKING A BIT TOO HAPPY."

WHY DID THE PROSTITUTE CROSS THE ROAD? TO GET TO THE OTHER SIDE, AND MAYBE PICK UP SOME BUSINESS ALONG THE WAY.

WHAT DO YOU CALL A FLY WITH NO WINGS? A WALK.

I TRIED TO IMPRESS MY DATE WITH A MAGIC TRICK. I MADE HER CLOTHES DISAPPEAR, BUT THEN I COULDN'T FIND THEM AGAIN.

MY DOCTOR TOLD ME I NEEDED TO BROADEN MY HORIZONS. SO I BOUGHT A WIDER TV.

I ASKED MY GIRLFRIEND IF SHE BELIEVED IN LOVE AT FIRST SIGHT. SHE SAID SHE'D NEED TO LOOK AT MY BANK ACCOUNT FIRST.

WHY DID THE POLICE
OFFICER GIVE THE
PROSTITUTE A WARNING?
BECAUSE SHE WAS
CAUSING A DISTURBANCE
WITH HER LOUD
"NEGOTIATIONS."

MY SIGNIFICANT OTHER SAID THEY NEEDED MORE SPACE. I SUGGESTED THEY TRY GOING OUTSIDE, BUT THEY STILL WEREN'T HAPPY.

What's the difference between a sadist and a masochist? A sadist is someone who likes to hurt others. A masochist is someone who likes to be hurt. A sadomasochist is someone who likes to hurt a masochist.

I TRIED TO TELL A JOKE ABOUT A VACUUM CLEANER, BUT IT JUST SUCKED.

WHY DID THE GOLFER WEAR TWO PAIRS OF PANTS? IN CASE HE GOT A HOLE IN ONE.

MY THERAPIST TOLD ME I HAVE A GOD COMPLEX. I TOLD HIM I'D PREFER A BIGGER OFFICE.

OUR POPULAR BOOKS

Jokes for Teenagers

"Jokes for Teenagers" is the ultimate joke book for ages 12-16, packed with over 50 pages of hilarious jokes, mini laugh challenges, and creative activities like writing your own punchlines.

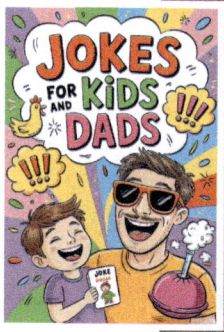

Jokes for Kids and Dads

Get ready to laugh louder, bond closer, and brighten every day with Jokes for Kids and Dads!
Perfect for kids aged 7-13 and their awesome dads, this hilarious collection packs over 44 jokes designed to make family time unforgettable – whether it's silly lunchtime surprises, family dinners, or quick car ride chuckles.

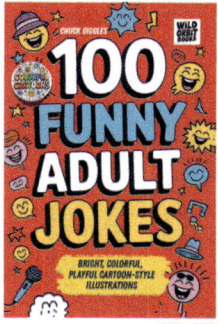

100 Funny Adult Jokes

100 Funny Adult Jokes – Clean, Hilarious Fun with Colorful Cartoons! Looking for a laugh-out-loud book that's perfect for teens, adults, and anyone who appreciates a good, clean joke? 100 Funny Adult Jokes delivers non-stop giggles and bonding moments with a hilarious collection of zingers, knock-knock jokes, one-liners ...

Buy now on Amazon

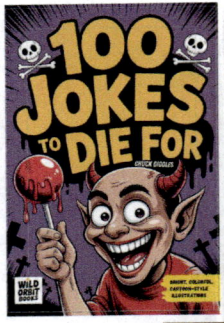

100 Jokes to die for

Dive into "100 Jokes to Die For," the ultimate collection of dark humor jokes designed exclusively for adults who appreciate wit as sharp as a surgeon's scalpel. Forget the stale, predictable humor; this book is packed with funniest jokes that walk the line between hilarious and delightfully inappropriate, ensuring a laugh-out-loud moment on every page.

Buy now on Amazon

Printed in Dunstable, United Kingdom